# ST EDMUND

## AND THE

## MONTAGU MONUMENTS

**LOTTERY FUNDED**

BUCCLEUCH
LIVING HERITAGE TRUST

THE PRINCE'S
REGENERATION TRUST

St Edmund's Parish Church
Warkton

Published in Great Britain in 2016 by Shire Publications Ltd (part of Bloomsbury Publishing Plc), PO Box 883, Oxford, OX1 9PL, UK.

1385 Broadway, 5th Floor New York, NY 10018, USA.

E-mail: shire@shirebooks.co.uk www.shirebooks.co.uk

A CIP catalogue record for this book is available from the British Library.

ISBN-13: 978 1 78442 163 2

PDF e-book ISBN: 978 1 78442 164 9

ePub ISBN: 978 1 78442 165 6

Layouts by Myriam Bell Design and typeset in Avenir.

Printed in Slovenia by Global Printing Solutions Group.

16 17 18 19 20    10 9 8 7 6 5 4 3 2 1

## ACKNOWLEDGEMENTS

Author: Louise Allen
This publication would not have been possible without the contributions of the following:

Alex Hatt, Paul Gardner, Rosie Fraser, the team at the Princes Regeneration Trust, Gareth Fitzpatrick, Honor Gay, Crispin Powell, Jana Schuster, Steven Ragdale and the team at The Buccleuch Living Heritage Trust, Tom Arber for photographing the monuments, Paul Wooles, Dr David Carrington and Skillingtons, Alan Frost, Alan Toseland, Tobit Curtis, Edward Lamb, Michael Jeans, Ian Wilson and The Parochial Church Council of St Edmund's Warkton, Helen Bates, Emma Purcell, Tamar Moore, Professor Phillip Lindley, Kezzabelle Ambler, Tricia Kirby, Gail Christie, Julia Thorley, Shusha Walmsley, Angela Gaye, Kate Beresford, Valentin Johnston, Gethin Williams, Kate Campbell, Holly Burns, Melissa Bradbury, Grace Fraser, Elize Rose, Sophie Wright, Mrs Hill, Mrs Blakely and Mrs Clubley and the Staff at Hawthorn School, Lyn Hewitson and Kettering Buccleuch Academy and Anne-Marie Sandos – Learning and Outreach Officer, Montagu Monuments Project.

This publication was created with the support of The Heritage Lottery Fund.

It is part of the Montagu Monuments Conservation Project which was enabled by generous assistance from:

The Buccleuch Living Heritage Trust
The Heritage Lottery Fund
St Edmund's Parochial Church Council
The Finnis Scott Foundation
The Leche Trust
The Georgian Group

And many other supporters.

# CONTENTS

# FOREWORD

### RICHARD MONTAGU DOUGLAS SCOTT, DUKE OF BUCCLEUCH AND QUEENSBERRY KBE

There are many aspects to St Edmund's Warkton. It is at once a quintessential rural parish church, a thriving focus for its community with a lively congregation, and also the home of four sculptures that rank with the finest in Europe. This long-awaited guidebook attempts to do justice to all these different facets of the church, with the aim of helping visitors to understand its history and role in the village community.

It is particularly opportune that this guidebook appears after the cleaning and conservation of the Warkton monuments and the refurbishment of the chancel, a tremendous endeavour which absorbed a great deal of energy between 2014 and 2016. Working on the monuments with the Parochial Church Council over the last few years has brought a wonderful sense of shared purpose between the church and my family. Visitors can now enjoy the spectacular treasures and beauty of the chancel as our ancestors would have done two hundred years ago, with the benefit of modern heating and lighting. Every time I visit the church, I relish the contrast between the simplicity of the nave and the rococo exuberance of the chancel.

Warmest congratulations are due to the many people and organisations who made the conservation of the monuments and the guidebook possible. They are listed on page 2. I hope that you thoroughly enjoy your time here and encourage your friends to visit.

*The Duke of Buccleuch and Queensberry.*

# INTRODUCTION

Throughout this guidebook there are short extracts of poems and prose inspired by the church and the monuments. These were written by children from Hawthorn Primary School and local adults who took part in creative writing workshops. Their words are inspired by their time spent in the church and in contemplating the monuments. They are included to share something of the emotion, tranquillity and beauty they experienced. For the full pieces please visit the Montagu Monuments page on The Buccleuch Living Heritage website.

*Students of Hawthorn School looking at the monuments.*

# THE HISTORY OF THE CHURCH

Today, St Edmund's reflects the evolution of an English church to meet the changing needs of its parishioners. A church has probably stood on this site since Anglo-Saxon times and the village's name seems to come from a person named Weorca, and 'tun' which means farm. A clerestory window, plastered over in the nineteenth century, is the only relic of this era, but re-used Roman tiles built into the masonry above the tower arch suggest an even earlier building.

The Normans built the nave and aisles in the twelfth century, and probably a chancel and tower as well, although the heavily restored arches are all that remain from this period. A chancel was built between the thirteenth and fifteenth centuries and, when its final fragment, the arch, was removed in 1872, traces of medieval painting could still be seen.

Patterns of worship change and architectural styles develop: at Warkton the aisles and clerestory were rebuilt in the fourteenth century and the tower was added between 1420 and 1450 in late Perpendicular style.

The Reformation left no mark on today's church, although the fourteenth-century piscina (a basin for washing communion vessels) in the wall of the south aisle suggests that there had once been a side chapel there. The manor itself passed into lay hands for the first time, given to Sir Edward Montagu in 1541.

The church was largely untouched during the religious upheavals of the Tudor period and of the seventeenth-century Commonwealth. The only evidence of disruption is the absence of marriage records from the registers between 1653 and 1658, when civil marriage became law.

The 1st Duke of Montagu (1638–1709) added a family mausoleum against the north side of the chancel, but it was not until 1748 that more radical changes were made in accordance with the eighteenth-century approach to worship. The altar was no longer the focal point as preaching – and therefore the pulpit – assumed new prominence and lengthy sermons meant more seating, allocated according to status. The church was fitted out with a triple-decker pulpit, box pews, a classical-style font and a musicians' gallery against the tower. The nave and aisle windows were remodelled, the window at the end of the south aisle blocked up and ceilings were installed. After the 2nd Duke died in 1749, the rebuilding of the chancel meant that the altar was effectively cut off from the worshippers in the nave.

In 1865, the energetic Henry Stobart was installed as Rector, bringing with him a zeal for changing and re-invigorating worship. On 9th February 1868, after only

*In an ancient landscape sits this ancient church that has known many secrets; shared the lives and the loves of the living — the ones who built it on this hill, in this place. Holds sacred moments of life captured in marble within its grey stones in such stillness.*

*— Tricia Kirby, Writers' Retreat participant*

ten weeks' work and an expenditure of £500, the transformed church was revealed. The box pews, the high pulpit and the gallery were removed; the Georgian chancel arch was replaced with one in medieval style; a new altar table and rails were installed and the iron grilles around the monuments were taken down. The ancient font bowl was found and re-installed on a new base on a re-paved floor that had been lowered by 6 inches in the nave and aisles.

In 1872, the Rector launched the second phase of his transformation. The south aisle was enlarged and re-roofed, the south porch was rebuilt and a vestry built against the south side of the chancel. The eighteenth-century windows in the south aisle and clerestory were rebuilt in medieval style and the

*The organ installed in the chancel in 1877 was removed in 1970.*

blocked-up fifteenth-century window exposed, revealing the remains of medieval wall paintings on the surrounding stonework. Over the next two years the ceilings were removed from the north aisle, the remaining eighteenth-century windows were replaced, the nave and aisles were re-roofed and new doors were installed.

This revitalisation of the interior stimulated generous donations: in 1877 a new organ was placed in the chancel, effectively concealing the monuments on the southern side; two new bells were hung in 1887; and choir stalls were added in 1901. The choir stalls were re-fashioned to form an organ gallery at the west end of the nave in the 1970s, allowing the chancel to be unobstructed.

By the late twentieth century St Edmund's, like all parish churches, was adapted again to: allow for more flexible forms of worship; accommodate the Sunday School; provide for increasing community use; and administrative requirements of a modern parish. In 1996–97, under the guidance of the Rectors Jack Wardle and Martin Perris, assisted by the Reverend Glynn Morgan (non-stipendary minister in charge of St Edmund's), extensions were built on either side of the tower. Designed by architect Alan J. Frost, these house a cloakroom, office and the Warren Room, watched over by the fine stained glass window by Jean-Baptiste Capronnier. The extensions were dedicated by the Bishop of Peterborough.

*The stained glass window in the Warren Room by Capronnier (1875) was moved there in 1997.*

*Renovations to the south side of the church in 1872.*

## CHURCH TIMELINE

| | |
|---|---|
| **946** | The king gives the manor to Earl Aelfgar |
| **Pre-1066** | Saxon church built |
| **c.1066** | Queen Maud gives the manor to the abbey of Bury St Edmunds |
| **c.1200** | Chancel and nave rebuilt in Early English style |
| **c.1300** | Aisles and clerestory rebuilt |
| **1420–50** | Tower built in Perpendicular style |
| **1541** | Manor granted to Sir Edward Montagu, Chief Justice of the King's Bench |
| **1558** | Church registers begin |
| **1638** | Tenor bell cast by Hugh Watts of Leicester |
| **1748** | Twelfth-century arches and chancel arch rebuilt; 2nd Duke of Montagu enlarges family vault and installs box pews, triple-decker pulpit, musicians' gallery and font |
| **1753–55** | Demolition of medieval chancel and new chancel built; monuments to 2nd Duke and Duchess installed |
| **1761** | Bell cast by Thomas Eyre of Kettering |
| **1781** | Monument to 3rd Duchess installed; second bell cast by Thomas Eyre |

| | |
|---|---|
| 1816 | Medieval font bowl found in a field |
| 1827 | Monument to Elizabeth, Duchess of Buccleuch installed |
| 1856 | Anglo-Saxon clerestory window found |
| 1866 | Extra rates required to enlarge the churchyard |
| 1867 | Vestry meeting to discuss alterations to the church |
| 1867 | Planning begins for restoration and alterations directed by Revd. Stobart |
| 1868 | Parish collection raises £50 for new pews and pulpit |
| 1872 | Vestry built |
| 1877 | Mrs Wells donates organ |
| 1888 | Mrs Wells donates two new bells celebrating Queen Victoria's Jubilee |
| 1901 | Mrs Wells donates choir stalls in memory of Thomas Jones (d.1898) |
| 1913 | Mr Ward (the organist) applies for an increase in salary, but church funds too low so charge of 3d to view the monuments imposed |
| 1915 | South porch re-dedicated by Bishop of Peterborough after woman found there with her dead infant |

*Above:* A photograph of the north side of the church taken in 1904.

*Right:* Extending the heating system in 1930.

*The Princess Royal's visit to St Edmund's church in 1938.*

| | |
|---|---|
| **1920** | Child's skeleton found during widening of path to west of churchyard and decently reburied |
| **1920** | War Memorial unveiled |
| **1930** | Nave floor replaced with stone flags and new heating system installed; stone coffin of woman with perfectly preserved hair found; school children excavate rubble to remove bone fragments for decent burial |
| **1938** | Princess Royal visits the church |
| **1955** | St Edmund's clock fails |
| **1965** | Restoration of tower and new clock |
| **1977** | Organ moved from chancel to gallery; choir stalls removed |
| **1990** | New roof drainage system installed; human bones unearthed and reburied near the south wall |
| **1993** | Sixth bell installed to honour Northamptonshire men and women who served in the Royal Signals |
| **1996/7** | Extensions built either side of the tower; stained glass window by Capronnier moved from south aisle to Warren Room |
| **2000** | First John Warren Foundation lecture |
| **2014** | The Montagu monuments restored |

*The restoration of the clock tower and installation of the new clock in 1965.*

# EXPLORING THE CHURCH

Entering St Edmund's through the south porch, the immediate impression is one of light flooding in from the vast east window and the simplicity of the clean lines created by Stobart's alterations in the 1860s and 1870s.

*Huge piles of beautifully shaped silky snow,*
*Formed like lush, sweet, giant marshmallows,*
*Ice white, feathery pillows cold to the touch.*
*Death shows in a ghostly statue whilst birds whistle.*

*— Gethin Williams, Hawthorn Primary School*

The font stands near the door, with the original medieval bowl set on a new base in 1868. It had been rescued from use as an animal drinking trough and before that as a water container in the village smithy.

In the south aisle is the piscina, and on the east wall a memorial to Thomas Johnson who died in 1657 aged 26, the inscription ending 'TO EDEN HEES TRANSPLANTED'.

*Floor plan of the church created by architect Alan Frost.*

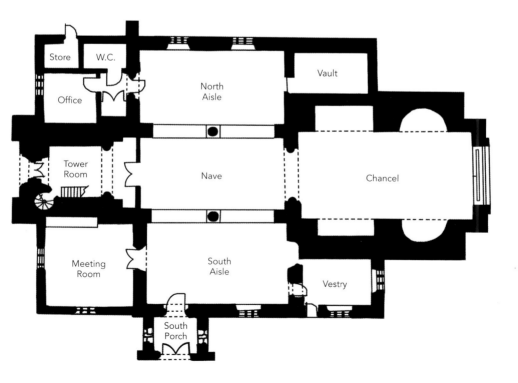

*The East windows allows light into the chancel to light up the monuments.*

The window surround at the east end of the aisle shows traces of a medieval wall painting uncovered during the 1860s restoration. When first revealed it was identifiable as a depiction of Shadrach, Meshach, and Abednego, cast into the fiery furnace (Book of Daniel, Chapter 3).

From the chancel steps there is a view through the east window to the churchyard beyond. This frames the limestone cross of the War Memorial (Grade II listed), unveiled on Passion Sunday, 28th March 1920 by Flight Lieutenant Harold Whistler, DSO, DFC, a Royal Flying Corps ace and son of the Reverend A.J. Whistler, much-loved Rector 1910–1920 and former Royal Navy chaplain.

On the northern side of the steps stands the elegant limestone and marble pulpit, which replaced the Georgian three-decker in 1868. In the north aisle there are small medieval stone heads moved during the

*Memorial to Hannah Payne, died 1759.*

The grand pulpit for preaching was installed in 1868.

restoration and the memorial to Mrs Hannah Payne, 'A woman of ... most amicable Behaviour...' (d.1759).

Looking west from the nave, there is a good view of the organ of 310 pipes, made by J.W. Walker & Sons of London and donated by Mrs A.E. Wells, a generous local benefactress to the church. It was moved from the chancel to its current position in the 1970s.

A ringing chamber was created at the same time. The church now has a peal of six bells, the earliest dating from 1638, 1718 and 1761. Two more were donated by Mrs Wells for the Golden Jubilee in 1887. The sixth bell was bequeathed in 1993 by the Knight family to honour the men and women of Northamptonshire who served in the Royal Signals regiment.

The bells were retuned in 1993.

In 1875 a painted glass window by Jean-Baptiste Capronnier was unveiled at the western end of the south aisle, with portraits of the Stobart family amongst Biblical figures. It was moved to the Warren Room in 1997 with funding from the John Warren Foundation.

# COMMUNITY –
# THE CHURCH AND ITS PEOPLE

### THE FAMILIES OF WARKTON

The parish registers, almost continuous since 1558, and the fine carved gravestones dating from 1728, delineate the history of the inhabitants of this small parish – families of farmers, craftspeople and agricultural workers. The west and south sections of churchyard have the finest examples of gravestones, of which 259 still stand.

Warkton has always been a small village – the population in 1921 was 192, and in 2011 it was 136. A church census of 1851 shows an attendance of 50 at morning service and 120 at the afternoon service, with 57 Sunday-school scholars.

There are many families who can trace three or more generations buried in the churchyard. The Bagshaw, Lamb and Toseland names recur from the nineteenth century with representatives still living in the village today. Names found in the registers from the sixteenth to the nineteenth centuries include Cave, Greene, Brampton and Meadowes and the families of Mutton, Panther, Taylor, Turner and Rowthorne who lived in Warkton for almost as long.

*Memorial to Reverend Lamotte.*

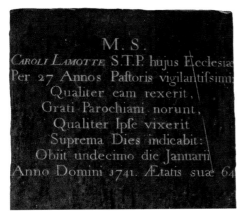

M.S.
CAROLI LAMOTTE S.T.P. hujus Ecclesiæ
Per 27 Annos Pastoris vigilantissimi
Qualiter eam rexerit,
Grati Parochiani norunt,
Qualiter Ipse vixerit
Suprema Dies indicabit:
Obiit undecimo die Januarii
Anno Domini 1741. Ætatis suæ 64

### THE RECTORS

Records of the priests in charge of Warkton stretch back to John de Thurmmeston in 1224, giving the first documentary evidence for the church.

Little is known of the personality of these clergymen before Charles

Lamotte, Rector 1714–41. He was Chaplain to the 1st Duke of Montagu and was appointed as rector in 1732. He was close to John, 2nd Duke, for whom he served as his eyes and ears in the parish. This role, and his neglect of property granted to him by the Duke, did not endear him to his parishioners. His memorial slab is on the east wall of the south aisle.

Most significant in creating the appearance of the church today was Henry Stobart, Rector 1865–81. Before his appointment Henry Stobart travelled as tutor to Lord Henry Scott, later 1st Lord Montagu of Beaulieu, son of the 5th Duke of Buccleuch, on a voyage to Australia and the South Pacific in 1852–56. His watercolour sketches, letters and 'lively journal' are held by the University of Queensland.

*Reverend Henry Stobart (1865–81). The impact of his alterations can still be seen.*

The Reverend Stobart was a follower of the 'high churchmen' of the Oxford Movement. He was popular with his parishioners and was the driving force in the restoration and remodelling of St Edmund's to fit it for worship in the mid-nineteenth century, personally donating one fifth of the money needed. In this restoration he was ably supported by George Warren Lamb, a solicitor and ancestor of present-day churchwarden Edward Lamb, whose family has had continuous links to the church for almost two hundred years.

Henry Stobart founded *The Almanac* in 1867. This village chronicle was produced annually until 1909 and recorded church, parish and family events. These volumes paint a vivid picture of Warkton life – economic and social change, public education, the growth of local industry and the effect of the growth of nearby Kettering on the village.

More recently the Reverends Jack Wardle, Martin Perris and Glynn Morgan provided leadership in adapting the church to the needs of the modern community in the 1970s and 1990s, and the commitment of Reverend Mark Lucas was key in enabling the restoration of the Montagu monuments in 2014.

# INTRODUCING THE MONUMENTS

Other than the rebuilt chancel there is no external clue that St Edmund's contains an exceptional grouping of four funerary monuments, three of which are of national, if not international, importance. Created by master sculptors – Louis François Roubiliac, Pieter Mathias van Gelder and Thomas Campbell – they are memorials to the last three generations of the Montagu family of nearby Boughton House.

The two monuments by Roubiliac to John, 2nd Duke of Montagu, and Mary, 2nd Duchess of Montagu (1755) are stunning examples of rococo design at its finest and their installation necessitated the rebuilding of the medieval chancel, creating a magnificent setting for further monuments.

Their daughter Mary Montagu, whose husband became the 3rd Duke, is commemorated by a dramatic and theatrical monument (1781) by van Gelder set in a niche in the style of Robert Adam. Finally, Campbell's monument to Elizabeth, Duchess of Buccleuch (1827) presents a dignified and formal image of the eighty-four-year-old matriarch of her family.

*A fish-eye image of the chancel, showing the monuments.*

Concerns about their condition led to major works in 2014 to clean, repair and stabilise the monuments and they can now be appreciated perhaps better than ever before. They are now in the ownership of The Buccleuch Living Heritage Trust.

*Sounding like a distant echo from the past,*
*Like a perfect chiselled cloud.*
*The statues smell like lavender scented garlands*
*Intermingled with salty tears.*

*— Holly Burns, Hawthorn Primary School*

## THE CHANCEL REMODELLED

When Duke John died in 1749 the church had a medieval chancel in Early English style, on the north side of which the 1st Duke had built 'a place of sepulture', or mausoleum.

John's monument was to be placed in a niche by the entrance to the vault. By the time Roubiliac had finished the sculpture the Duchess had also died and there were plans to demolish the southwest corner of the chancel to house her monument. However, in June 1753 the work revealed that the old chancel was so decayed that the only option was to demolish it and rebuild.

By July 1755 the chancel was complete. The two monuments, guarded by iron 'palisades', were in place and two further empty

*During the arch restoration, decoration at the top of the pillars was damaged, resulting in different decoration at the top of both pillars.*

niches created, all lit by the massive east window and separated from the nave by iron gates.

The demolition of the Georgian chancel opening exposed the original pointed arch to be in poor condition and so it was replaced in medieval style. In the restoration of 1867–68 the ironwork was removed but the introduction of a new organ and choir stalls obscured the monuments, which were only fully revealed again in 1970.

During the restoration of Duke John's monument fragments of fourteenth- and fifteenth-century stone mouldings, probably from the old chancel, were discovered in the structure's core.

*The core of Duke John's monument included fragments from the medieval chancel.*

# JOHN, 2ND DUKE OF MONTAGU (1690–1749)

A most amiable man and one of the most feeling I ever knew.
– Horace Walpole

In 1705, aged fifteen, John married Mary, fourth daughter of John Churchill, Duke of Marlborough, thus acquiring a national hero as father-in-law and the difficult Sarah Jennings, the Duchess, as mother-in-law. He travelled to Flanders to the campaign against Louis XIV.

John became 2nd Duke in 1709 aged nineteen. He had many interests and passions. Although his marriage to Mary was a political alliance they later became devoted. Tragically, their three sons died young, leaving daughters Isabella and Mary.

John was fascinated by the technical aspects of warfare and was appointed Master-General of the Ordnance. He also achieved the army rank of General. In 1722 he petitioned the King to allow him to establish a colony on St Lucia and St Vincent in the Caribbean: his efforts ended in expensive failure.

In his public life he was an antiquarian, philanthropist and had links with Thomas Coram, founder of the London Foundling Hospital.

Privately his enthusiasms were distinctive and endearing but his mother-in-law was scathing about his practical jokes: 'All my son-in-law's talents lie in things only natural in boys of fifteen, and he is now about two and fifty.' Nicknamed 'Duke John the Planter', he established extensive avenues of trees in Warkton and surrounding parishes.

*Duke John's portrait. The Tower of London, his place of office as Master of Ordnance, is in the background.*

John held enlightened views for the time on the education of black people, typified by his paying for the education of Francis Williams, a free black man from Jamaica. He also championed Job Ben Solomon (Ayuba Suleiman Diallo), brought to London from slavery in 1733. When Diallo returned to Senegal he wrote, 'praying God to bless you for what you have done for me.'

He met Ignatius Sancho, an African who went on to be a writer and composer, who was then a young servant-boy in Greenwich. He took Sancho under his wing, taking him into his household and sponsoring his education. The relationship between Sancho and the Montagus was to last for generations.

John was devoted to animals, as reported by Horace Walpole:

[His will has] two codicils, one in favour of his servants, and the other of his dogs, cats and creatures ... one of his cats jumped

In memory
of
JOHN DUKE of MONTAGU
who died July 5 1749 aged 59

His afflicted widow
MARY DUTCHESS of MONTAGU
erects this monument

on his knee, 'what,' says he, 'have you a mind to be a witness too! You can't for you are a party concerned.'

He refused to have animals destroyed, maintained a hospital for farm animals and rescued a toothless old lion. It 'must never be locked up at all, but go where he will…. To have boiled meat, no horse flesh, nor no bones given him. To lie every night in his house by the Old Pantry.'

## DUKE JOHN'S MONUMENT

*Portrait of Sarah Jennings, Mary Churchill's mother.*

John died in 1749, leaving £1,000 'for mourning'. He had considered a mausoleum in Boughton's park or a monument in Weekley but the Duchess decided instead to commission this memorial at Warkton and entrusted the details to Martin Folkes, President of the Royal Society and the Duke's friend.

*The Dublin Courant* reported in December 1749: 'Roubillac [sic] is preparing a noble monument to his Grace the Duke of Montagu, the Device of which is Charity erecting a Shrine to his memory and Fame applauding her.' Shortly afterwards Fame was replaced in the design by the figure of the Duchess. On 30th October 1754 *The Public Advertiser* noted that 'the erecting of two Superb Monuments, in the manner of Ancient Roman Temples,' was finished 'after more than 17 weeks labour.'

As we view the monument, we are spectators at its completion. The grieving Duchess leans on the base watching Charity hanging a portrait medallion of the Duke. She is helped by a small boy who leans down beside an urn as she supports another child in her left arm. The device of hanging the medallion is the earliest example of Roubiliac creating a sculpture within a sculpture, a theme he later returned to. At Charity's feet a weeping boy extinguishes a torch, indicating a life cut short.

**Opposite:**
*Monument to John 2nd Duke of Montagu by Roubiliac.*

A cannon and associated equipment projects from one side, and on the other a flag and Fame's trumpet reference John's rank of General and role as Master-General of the Ordnance. Despite the symbols of war and reputation, the theme of the monument is clearly Charity, the virtue for which the Duke was noted.

Below, his widow holds the Montagu coat of arms; a ducal coronet and the ribbon and badge of St George for the Order of the Garter, perhaps to be added to the monument, rather than being simply displayed.

The almost life-size white marble statues are set in a typically complex diagonal composition across and around the multi-coloured marble architectural elements, all framed within the chancel niche.

When the monuments to the Duke and Duchess were installed, the Duke's monument was found to be lower. The need to match the height to the Duchess's monument led to the addition at the top of a curved section surmounted by the classical feature of a 'firepan and Smoak'.

## THE ARTIST – LOUIS FRANÇOIS ROUBILIAC (c.1705–62)

Born and trained in Lyon, Roubiliac studied in Dresden with Balthasar Permoser, a former student of Bernini, and in Paris with Nicolas Coustou, a French Baroque sculptor.

All Roubiliac's known surviving works were executed in Britain, where he settled in c.1730 with his Huguenot wife, and he is generally considered, together with Michael Rysbrack, to be one of the most important sculptors working in eighteenth-century England. His career was critical in establishing the status of sculptors as creative designers rather than as artisanal sculptor-masons.

He specialised in portrait busts and funerary monuments and was renowned for his handling of marble, particularly the light and flowing lines of his figures, subtle surface textures and lively asymmetrical composition, all typical of the French rococo style.

George Vertue, the English engraver and antiquary, wrote:

> ... [the] greatness of [Roubiliac's] genius in his invention, design and execution, [is] in every part equal, if not superior, to any others... his models of statues, monuments, bustos [sic] are very curious and excellent, with great skill and variety. His inventions very copious and fre [sic] – picturesque – so light and easy – as painting.

Roubiliac's first independent commission was a statue of Handel for Vauxhall Gardens in 1737. A year later he opened his own studio and became, as an article in the *Telegraph* (14 February 2016) put it, 'The go-to sculptor for the celebrity portrait.'

In addition to these larger commissions Roubiliac executed vivid portrait busts, which were admired for their perceptive depiction of the sitter's character, in particular busts of William Hogarth and Alexander Pope.

Roubiliac was paid £1,800 for the Warkton commission and he may have been chosen for it because of his monument of the Duke of Argyll in Westminster Abbey, completed in 1749, the year Duke John died. It is regarded as one of his greatest works, although his monument to Lady Elizabeth Nightingale (1761), also in the Abbey, is better known. A year later another much-praised work may also have influenced the decision: in a letter to Lord Hardwicke, September 1750, Thomas Birch wrote, 'Roubillac is the Sculptor who has gain'd new reputation by the Mo[nu]ment of general wade.'

*From their masons' yard they travel north a hundred miles to serve the great and good whose birthright blesses them with wealth and power enough to make them immortal.*

*And there in a country church, those characters, careers, and charitable deeds are commemorated for posterity...*

*– Gail Christie, Writers' Retreat participant*

# MARY CHURCHILL, 2ND DUCHESS OF MONTAGU, (1689–1751)

Mary was the fourth daughter of John Churchill, Duke of Marlborough, the great national hero and victor of the War of Spanish Succession, and Sarah, 1st Duchess of Marlborough, the strong-willed friend and confidante of Queen Anne.

Mary married John Montagu in 1705 when she was sixteen and he fifteen. The marriage was a coup for her father-in-law, Ralph, Earl of Montagu, and was instrumental in Ralph securing his own dukedom in the same year. John succeeded his father in 1709.

Mary's letters reveal her to be quick-witted and strong-willed, with firm opinions. A letter to her mother in 1716, for example, condemns Paris as dirty, smelly and containing nothing much of interest.

*Opposite:*
*Monument to Mary Churchill, 2nd Duchess of Montagu by Roubiliac.*

*Below: Portrait of Mary Churchill.*

Her relations with her mother were always strained; perhaps, as her father thought, they were too much alike. By 1720 they were hardly speaking and two years later Mary wrote to her father complaining of her mother's treatment of her, possibly just before his death. For her part Sarah wrote an account of how she considered her daughters had behaved badly towards her and circulated it amongst her friends. A partial reconciliation was achieved just before Sarah's death.

Mary was independent enough to travel abroad without her husband, which was unusual at the time. When in England she was usually in London at Montagu House in Bloomsbury until, in the early 1730s, John commissioned a new Montagu House in Whitehall. She also used a property at Blackheath.

She had a reputation for enjoying London's social life and entertainments, preferring it to

MARY
DUTCHESS of MONTAGU,
Widow of IOHN DUKE of MONTAGU,
Daughter of IOHN DUKE of MARLBOROUGH,
died may 14 MDCCLI.
aged 61.

A pious remembrance of the best of mothers
MARY COUNTESS of CARDIGAN
erects this monument.

life in the family's various country houses and estates, leaving the running of these houses to Duke John.

## MARY CHURCHILL'S MONUMENT

The 2nd Duchess died in May 1751, before work was complete on Duke John's memorial and supervision was taken over by her daughter Mary, Countess of Cardigan, who added the further commission to Roubiliac for this monument, 'In pious remembrance of the best of mothers'.

The work was completed by December 1753, transported to Warkton in June 1754 and erected in October.

The grey marble monument rises in stages to a large urn standing in a niche designed to give a *trompe l'oeil* effect of depth. A small boy at its foot, and a small girl on top, are in the act of draping a garland of flowers around the urn so that, as with Duke John's monument, the spectator is witnessing the final stages of its erection.

Below, three young women symbolising the Fates are posed in a typically dynamic rococo zigzag composition. The three Fates were sisters – incarnations of destiny, life and death – who would visit three days after a birth to determine the length of the child's life. Clotho, the Spinner, makes the thread for the Tapestry of Life and is depicted top left with her distaff. Lachesis, the Allotter, who draws the lots and measures the thread – or length – of life, sits opposite her and Atropos, the Inflexible, who cuts the thread with her shears, stands below to the left. A hank of twine found behind the monument may have represented the thread itself.

Traditionally described as old women, impartial, stern and severe, here they are shown as young, beautiful and emotionally engaged with the drama.

Atropos has a skull under her left hand, the symbol of Death, on which Clotho rather casually rests her feet. Lachesis holds up

*Through a tear in the veil of time,*
*We see these marbled souls*
*Poised in the glimmering light of eternity,*
*Where the thread of life has been cut...*

*— Shusha Walmsley, Writers' Retreat participant*

her hand, apparently dismayed, as the thread is cut short. The fabrics of their clothing – striped wool, fustian and linen – are subtly depicted in the carving of the marble.

On the lowest step is a child holding the spindle from which the thread has been cut. He seems unaware of the tragedy that has just occurred as he stares out towards Duke John's monument, a device that increases the feeling of pathos. During restoration it was noted that the boy was in a brighter marble than the rest of the figures, perhaps to ensure that this important symbolic element was visible through the original protective screens.

# MARY MONTAGU, 3RD DUCHESS OF MONTAGU (1712–1775)

*Below:*
*Mary Montagu, 3rd Duchess of Montagu by Thomas Gainsborough.*

*Overleaf:*
*Monument to Mary Montagu, 3rd Duchess of Montagu, by Van Gelder.*

Mary was the younger daughter of John, 2nd Duke of Montagu and Mary Churchill. She had no surviving brothers and, after her sister Isabella made a second marriage to an Irishman, rumoured to be a fortune-hunter, she became the favoured child and heiress to the larger part of her father's property.

In 1730 Mary married 'the boy next door', George Brudenell, 4th Earl of Cardigan, from the neighbouring estate of Deene.

George adopted the name Montagu and they mounted a long campaign to restore the 'Montagu honours' – the title and the Garter – and in 1766 the Dukedom of Montagu was re-created by Act of Parliament.

The 3rd Duke and Duchess were established figures at the court of George III. George was Governor to the Prince of Wales and Governor of Windsor Castle; the King threatened abdication on one occasion when he was being pressured to replace him.

Here on th...
Thy widow...
Let me, O...
Inferibe t'...
To Birth e...
Thou did...
for in th...
All Virtu...
Not CHA...
More Pit...
To ev'ry...
Gave Rain...
No wond...
Poor orp...
Heav'n g...
But The...

id with Tears
m rears
MONTAGU
s due
oble Friend
, but lend
Mind
s shind
nder
treft
al

> *...Knitted, knotted and twisted,*
> *The thread continues.*
> *A long journey can cause it to fray*
> *Breaking when time wears it out...*
>
> — *Angela Gaye, Writers' Retreat participant*

Mary and Isabella fell out over the inheritance and Mary abandoned Boughton House because of the resulting legal dispute. She may have been naturally disputatious, for Horace Walpole described a ball where 'Lady Cardigan had so many quarrels on hand that very few of her friends were present...'.

She and her husband were great collectors and travelled extensively on the Continent, sending back Old Masters, furniture and bronzes. In France in 1756 they acquired seven significant paintings, including Leonardo's *Madonna of the Yarn Winder* and El Greco's *Adoration of the Shepherds*.

Mary patronised many contemporary artists, and was herself an artist in pastels. She was painted by Gainsborough and Reynolds and gave commissions to the Huguenot cabinet-maker Pierre Langlois, and the carver Jean Antoine Cuenot. Her connoisseurship must have stood her in good stead in the commissioning of the monument to her mother by Roubiliac.

Mary and George had four children. Two daughters died young and the only son, John, Marquis of Monthermer, died aged thirty-five, unmarried. He was a knowledgeable collector, purchasing many art works on a nine-year-long Grand Tour from 1751. Their surviving daughter Lady Elizabeth married Henry, 3rd Duke of Buccleuch.

Mary was known for her many charitable acts, especially in support of widows and orphans, as the imagery of her monument shows. She inherited her father's liberal views and fostered the education and career of Ignatius Sancho, taking him into her household as valet, then butler. The family were subscribers to his book and commissioned him to write music. When he became too unwell to continue to work for them Mary helped him by leaving him a legacy that enabled him to set up a grocery shop. He became a composer, businessman and the first black person of African origin to vote in a British Parliamentary election.

# MARY MONTAGU'S MONUMENT

Mary died in 1775 and her monument by Pieter Mathias van Gelder was commissioned by her widower George in September 1777. It was completed in September 1781.

The scene is set on one level on a grey marble stage, placed within an architectural niche. There is no documentary evidence for the suggestion, made in the early twentieth century, that the niche was designed by Robert Adam. However, his influence is obvious, which is unsurprising as van Gelder frequently worked with the architect.

The apsidal recess has pairs of fluted pilasters with Ionic capitals flanking three oval reliefs of classically dressed women. The central figure holds an inverted torch signifying death and the flanking reliefs show a needlewoman and a female artist, identifying two of the Duchess's interests 'suitable' for a noblewoman.

The free-standing figures advance more towards the viewer than they do in the earlier monuments and the use of coloured marble is limited to the figures, the apse in white contrasting with the grey of the 'stage' and a black band echoing the black marble border to the chancel's paving.

A central neo-classical urn on a drum base bears a verse by Henry Lyte. He had accompanied Mary's son John on his Grand Tour and was responsible for overseeing the monument's commissioning.

To the left of the urn an angel, whose billowing robes show that he has just alighted, points heavenwards as if to reassure the seated woman who collapses despairingly against the urn. A boy at her feet wipes away a tear and gestures towards the ducal coronet against her skirts.

It has been suggested that this is the Duchess with the coronet nestling against her skirts as an indication of her rank. On the other hand she was sixty-three at the time of her death and it may

*Royally worn the coronet of old,*
*Fruitful colours in a field of gold.*
*Flowing waterfall of velvet so grand,*
*Radiant beams seen throughout the land.*

*— Elize Rose, Hawthorn Primary School*

well be that this young woman, who has been suckling the infant cradled in her left arm, is actually a widow, distraught at the loss of a lady notable for her charitable support of widows and orphans. Henry Lyte's verse includes words that seem to describe this scene:

> Poor orphan Babes and Widows mourn,
> Heav'n gains a Holy saint 'tis true
> But They have lost their MONTAGU

The composition is completed with a draped, barefooted elderly woman, perhaps another widow, who is tenderly touching the infant's hand.

## THE ARTIST – PIETER MATHIAS VAN GELDER (c.1742–1827)

Pieter Mathias van Gelder was born in Amsterdam and details of his life are obscure until 1769, when he entered the London Royal Academy schools. He was also employed in the workshop of sculptor Thomas Carter II from the same year.

According to John Deare, one of Carter's apprentices, van Gelder was 'considered one of the best hands in London at foliage' – demonstrated by the monument to Mary Frampton in Moreton Church, Dorset which has been described as 'one of the most enchanting works of art in any English church' (Rupert Gunnis, 1968).

In 1775 he married Martha, daughter of the carpenter-architect Charles Evans for whom he carried out commissions. By 1776 he had his own premises in London.

Like other mason-sculptors, van Gelder was a building contractor and produced monumental and architectural sculpture, from fireplaces to funerary

*As I created, so I destroyed. More and more of my marble tabula rasa lay, chipped into shards around my feet as the strength of my arms gave birth to him. . . I simply half shut my eyes and felt his lines, his frame of stone with its lustrous opalesque flesh.*

*— Kate Beresford, Writers' Retreat participant*

monuments. He frequently collaborated with architect Robert Adam, executing various monuments to Adam's designs, including that to Major John André (d.1780) in Westminster Abbey.

Warkton was his most important commission, although how he obtained the work is unknown. He and his team also cleaned and repaired the Roubiliac monuments.

# ELIZABETH, DUCHESS OF BUCCLEUCH AND QUEENSBERRY (1743–1827)

The only surviving child of George, 3rd Duke of Montagu and Mary, daughter of John, 2nd Duke of Montagu, Elizabeth was a great heiress, inheriting substantial estates from her parents and her aunt Isabella, Lady Beaulieu.

*Elizabeth Buccleuch as a young woman by Thomas Gainsborough.*

She married Henry Scott, 3rd Duke of Buccleuch, in 1767 and moved to his family seat, Dalkeith Palace, near Edinburgh. The marriage was happy and to her husband she was 'the best wife, the best mother and the kindest friend that God ever created in this world.'

They had six surviving children. Of the sons, Charles (1772–1819) became 4th Duke of Buccleuch in 1812 on the death of his father while Henry became Lord Montagu. The four daughters all married well and Elizabeth was the centre of a large family.

'The Angel of Buccleuch' was famous for good works: she and the Duke were said to give £30,000 a year to charity. She supported the family of freed slave Ignatius Sancho, butler to her mother; aided French émigrés; and was sympathetic to physical disability, supporting the Blind Asylum and many hospitals, and helping poet Thomas Carley, born without hands. She was so well known for charity the Scottish artist William Bonnar's painting *The Benefactresses* depicts Elizabeth with her daughter-in-law Harriet, Countess of Dalkeith, visiting a widow and children

Despite payments such as 'different small sums to beggars' or 2s 6d to 'Mad Sally', her carefully researched giving was directed to helping people help themselves. She paid for the apprenticeship of Ignatius Sancho's son William as a bookbinder; also for an apprenticeship for the son of the estate steward at Beaulieu and medical training for the son of one of her tenants.

Elizabeth was an indefatigable traveller. On their Grand Tour she and the Duke travelled through France, Italy, Switzerland and along the Rhine. Her Roman itinerary was intensive, including fourteen churches in one day. In Britain she moved between London, her villa at Richmond and Scotland.

She purchased art from contemporary artists including Henri-Pierre Danloux, Thomas Lawrence and Scottish artists Alexander Nasmyth and Alexander Carse. Her collections included jewels, coins and medals; her library also reveals wide-ranging tastes. Elizabeth was interested in music and ballet, supported musicians and was responsible for assembling much of the music archive at Boughton House.

Elizabeth died aged eighty-four at Richmond. Sir Walter Scott wrote, 'She was a woman of unbounded beneficence to, and even beyond, the extent of her princely fortune. She had a masculine courage and a great firmness in enduring affliction...'.

*Opposite:*
*Monument to Elizabeth Buccleuch by Thomas Campbell.*

IN MEMORY OF

ELIZABETH MONTAGU

DUCHESS DOWAGER OF BUCCLEUCH AND QUEENSBERRY

WHO DIED ON THE XXI OF NOVEMBER MDCCCXXVII

AGED EIGHTY-THREE

HER GRATEFUL AND AFFECTIONATE GRANDSON

WALTER FRANCIS

DUKE OF BUCCLEUCH AND QUEENSBERRY

ERECTS THIS MONUMENT

THINE ALMS ARE HAD IN REMEMBRANCE IN THE SIGHT OF GOD

ACTS CHAP. X. VER. XI.

# ELIZABETH'S MONUMENT

In contrast to the other monuments in Warkton's chancel, the Duchess of Buccleuch's seems restrained, even sombre. Certainly it is far from theatrical. It was commissioned in 1827 from Thomas Campbell by her grandson Walter, the 5th Duke, as her son had predeceased her.

Campbell's task was to produce a memorial to a much-loved and respected widow of eighty-four and to symbolise her dignity, faith and virtues. He has done so by depicting her as a Roman matron, seated very upright on a chair placed centrally on a high plinth within an unadorned niche. Her modest draperies and dignified stance echo the classical depictions of virtuous Roman ladies, pillars of civic and domestic rectitude. Strangely, the image is very similar to Campbell's 1843 relief portrait of actress Sarah Siddons.

However, unlike the scroll that Sarah holds, Elizabeth's hands rest firmly on a large Bible, its cover bearing the letters IHS, the first three letters of the name of Jesus: in Greek capitals ΙΗΣΟΥΣ, or IHSOUS in Latin. This is the only clearly Christian symbol shown on any of the four monuments.

Elizabeth gazes out through the east window of the chancel, perhaps, as it has been suggested, towards Boughton House. Face-on her expression seems forbidding, but from the side she appears much softer, with a trace of the enchanting smile seen in Gainsborough's portrait of her in 1767 as a young bride.

The central plinth is flanked by two standing figures. To the viewer's left a female Scribe records her deeds and virtues on a scroll. Elizabeth had lived such a long life that the Scribe has already filled four scrolls which can be seen in the box behind her.

To the right a male figure, possibly Thanatos, holds the upended torch of her life, very long compared to those depicted on the other Warkton

*Take a closer look. Can you discern the subtler meanings in my work? Your knowledge of the Classics does you credit. How clever and wise you are. Let me say, that I, the creator of this monument, appreciate your part in its presentation.*

*— Julia Thorley, Writers' Retreat participant*

monuments, reflecting her great age. Thanatos is the Greek god of death, who is usually depicted with an upturned torch and with crossed legs. He wears a wreath of poppy seed heads. In ancient Greece and Rome poppies were used as offerings to the dead and on tombstones as a symbol of eternal sleep.

## THE ARTIST – THOMAS CAMPBELL (1790–1858)

Thomas Campbell was born in Edinburgh where he was apprenticed to a marble cutter. In 1816, his busts caught the attention of Gilbert Innes of Stow, Deputy Governor of the Bank of Scotland, 'the richest commoner in Scotland'. Innes became his patron and enabled him to study at the Royal Academy Schools in London. He was informally tutored by Joseph Nollekens, and worked as a journeyman for Edward Hodges Baily.

*Thomas Campbell's bust of the 5th Duke of Buccleuch at Bowhill.*

He moved to Rome in 1818 where he associated with Antonio Canova and Bertel Thorvaldsen. When he opened his own studio it became a fashionable resort for eminent visitors to Rome, many of whom he sculpted as portrait busts. His career was enhanced by the patronage of the 6th Duke of Devonshire, including a celebrated commission for a figure of Princess Pauline Borghese.

Campbell returned to London in 1829, retaining his Italian studio. He continued making portrait busts and a number of monuments, including a bronze of the Duke of York for the esplanade of Edinburgh Castle.

He was acquainted with the 5th Duke of Buccleuch before the Warkton commission, possibly having met him when the Duke made his Grand Tour.

# THE RESTORATION STORY

By the millennium, the Montagu monuments had stood in Warkton's chancel for over two hundred years, exposed to the slow fall of dust, the ravages of time, to accident and well-meaning attempts at cleaning.

Twentieth-century cleaning attempts and solid fuel heaters which emitted damaging pollutants, including sulphur dioxide, caused numerous problems, including the severe degradation of the marble sculptures and structural instability.

Even when the old stoves were replaced, weekly services and community use resulted in fluctuations in temperature and relative humidity that caused condensation on the delicate surfaces of the monuments, increasing the rate of decay.

Wing-tips and fingers had been accidentally knocked off, key sections were loose and the young boy at the foot of Mary Churchill, Duchess of Montagu's monument had lost his spindle.

The condition of English historic churches is assessed every five years, and after the 2006 survey the Parochial Church Council (PCC) commissioned a report by Skillingtons, a specialist conservation and restoration company. Their assessment identified structural instability as well as surface erosion, ingrained dust and minor damage. The message was clear: urgent work was needed.

It was also clear that saving and restoring the monuments would be a major undertaking, which had to be carried out whilst keeping the church open for regular worship and community use. Together the Parochial Church Council of St Edmund's, under the leadership of the Reverend Mark Lucas, and The Buccleuch Living Heritage Trust (BLHT) raised £500,000, including £318,000 from the Heritage Lottery Fund.

*Attempts to clean the statues in the twentieth century contributed to their degradation.*

Between February and November 2014 Skillingtons carried out the first professional conservation of the monuments since they were carved, working with a team that included the church architect, the Prince's Regeneration Trust and

representatives from the BLHT and the PCC. All the monuments required cleaning to remove impacted dirt, including spiders' webs, which are chemically harmful. Skillingtons used poultices, combining a wet inert material with an active chemical that drew out and dissolved contaminants and staining.

On 14 April 2015 a Service of Celebration was held in the church to mark the completion of the conservation work and thank the team for their impressive work.

The partners could not rest on their laurels – it was essential to understand how to maintain an environment that would

*Poultices were applied to the monuments to lift away the dirt.*

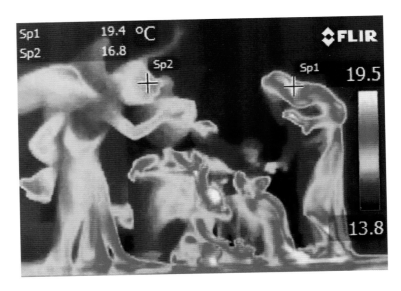

*A thermal image of Mary Montagu's monument showing the effects of solar gain on the statue and walls.*

conserve the monuments in their newly restored condition. Environmental control is challenging in historic churches, which are cold places, requiring heating during services and events leading to damaging atmospheric fluctuations. At St Edmund's the weekly heating for services caused humidity to rise, and then, as the church cooled again, condensation formed on the marble, leading to further deterioration. The solution was to even out these fluctuations by using localised conservation heating that lets the chancel cool down slowly. Preliminary monitoring of this approach is encouraging.

Conservation, management and maintenance plans now guide the care of the monuments and chancel and help to balance the needs of church users and monuments.

## THE RESTORATION PROCESS

### JOHN, 2ND DUKE OF MONTAGU

This monument was the most endangered. Corrosion of the internal ironwork holding the different elements together was expanding the fixings, jacking key elements out of place and

*Charity is lifted from the monument to be cleaned and have supports upgraded.*

lifting the Duchess half an inch above the marble platform. With a real risk of sculptures fracturing and falling the rusting ironwork had to be replaced.

The monument was dismantled, with 90 individual elements numbered to aid reconstruction. The major sculptures, the Duchess and Charity, were first lifted free with specially designed slings and hoists. Once removed, all the elements were cleaned and the corroded ironwork replicated in marine-grade stainless steel except where the figure of Charity was anchored by its original iron fixing, a 1.3-metre-long bar inserted into the core. This, the largest of all the ironwork, was sound and could be re-used.

The discovery that the monument's core included fragments from the medieval chancel was an exciting revelation. Dismantling also revealed that Roubiliac had used ingenious cost-cutting measures, including laminating thin layers of marble to cheaper limestone.

Finally, after reconstruction, the marble was buffed with wax and the gilded inscription restored.

## MARY CHURCHILL, 2ND DUCHESS OF MONTAGU

This monument was in good structural condition, although so coated with impacted dirt that colour and detail were lost. After dusting with soft brushes it was treated with poultices with dramatic results, revealing previously unseen details in the garland, the intricate hairstyles of the Fates, and the elements of skull, shears and spindle which bring the allegory to life.

The skull was loose from its plaster bed, making it vulnerable, and this was re-fixed. The spindle held by the small boy at the foot of the monument had gone missing during the twentieth century, damaging the iconography of the monument, but fortunately detailed images were discovered at The Courtauld Institute of Art, allowing a replacement to be carved in marble.

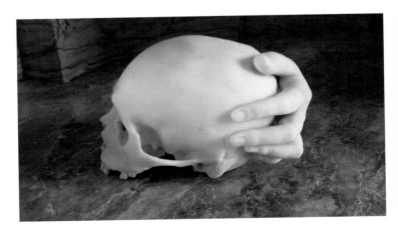

*Side view of the skull removed for cleaning*

## MARY, 3RD DUCHESS OF MONTAGU

The challenge with this monument was to work on the delicate statues, which sat on a fragile, hollow base. To reach the back of the figure group and the top of the architectural niche the restorers had to use a cantilevered scaffold, suspended above the base.

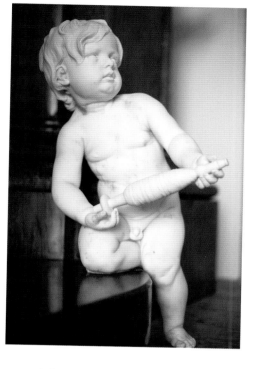

A misalignment was discovered between two slabs in the base, so this had to be dismantled and realigned to give a level floor. This area also showed evidence that the weeping boy and the coronet had been moved from their original positions; these were correctly replaced.

A number of the fine sculptural details had been broken over time. During the work the angel's upper right wingtip, the weeping boy's right forefinger, the widow's fifth left-hand finger and the top of the Duchess's left sandal were put back before finally the inscriptions were re-touched.

*The original spindle was lost. Photographs were found allowing the spindle to be remade.*

*Vulnerable parts that had broken off the statues were replaced during the restoration.*

*Protecting the elaborate monument to Mary Montagu required a cantilevered scaffold.*

## ELIZABETH MONTAGU, DUCHESS OF BUCCLEUCH

This monument was affected by 'sugaring', where the bonds of the crystalline structure of the marble are gradually dissolved like sugar by a chemical reaction. The left hand of the male figure was disintegrating dramatically, and other areas on both flanking figures were affected.

Two main options were debated. Restoration, which produces a more aesthetically pleasing result but entails the loss of some original fabric, would involve re-carving the hand, cutting back the arm to give a clean fit and then attaching the new piece. A conservation solution would have been to consolidate the original fabric, repairing the hand with resin and other synthetic materials, while retaining as much of the original sculpture as possible.

*Grand coronet regally perched upon my head,*
*Sitting tall.*
*Heavy, rich, velvety fabric but light as a feather.*
*Marble smooth edges satin to the touch...*

*— Grace Fraser, Hawthorn Primary School*

Fortunately, a 1947 photograph showed the hand in detail, allowing an accurate replacement to be carved in marble and fitted into place with a stainless steel pin. Polyester resin was used to conceal the joint while conservation work stabilised the remaining sugaring.

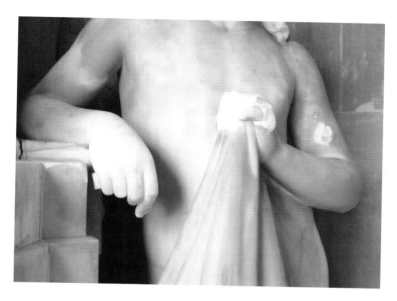

The male figure's hand on Elizabeth Buccleuch's monument is eaten away.

The restored hand.

# BRINGING THE
# MONUMENTS ALIVE

Alongside the work to preserve the monuments for future generations, in 2014–16 various activities took place to share the beauty and stories of the monuments with the wider community.

Young people of the Free Rangers after-school club at the Green Patch allotments in Kettering took part in creative workshops themed around the monuments.

A pop-up exhibition was held at the Grange Resource Centre at the Grange Estate in Kettering for people to find out more about the unique treasures nearby and enjoy some cake.

Students at Kettering Buccleuch Academy honed their life drawing skills by making detailed studies.

Young people at St Edmund's Church Sunday School found out more about the people remembered in the sculptures.

In May 2016, Deep Roots Tall Trees Choir and Musicians performed four songs that they had written especially for the monuments. Working with internationally acclaimed singer-songwriter Barb Jungr, members of the choir wrote and researched the songs, which were based on pieces either from the Montagu music collection or otherwise associated with the family.

Adults took part in a writers' retreat inspired by the monuments. Students of Hawthorn Primary School took part in a short course of workshops to write poems inspired by the monuments and the lives of John, Mary, Mary and Elizabeth which you have read throughout this book.

*The gentle smell of frankincense*
*Surrounds the ancient tomb.*
*Pearly cloth draping,*
*Shimmering in the moon.*

*— Sophie Wright, Hawthorn Primary School*